THE
Happen*Stance* Story

CHAPTER FOUR

Helena Nelson

Happen*Stance*

Narrative © Helena Nelson, 2010
Poems © individual authors
Cover image: *Portrait of the Artist as a Middle-Aged Woman*
© Gillian Beaton, 2006

ISBN 978-1-905939-40-4

All rights reserved

Acknowledgements:
Thanks to the Happen*Stance* subscribers and readers without whom this would not happen; to Ross Kightly, for helping with proof-reading; and last but not least to Tony Walker who got me to watch Kenneth Branagh's version of *Love's Labour's Lost* as a Hollywood musical.

Note: the graphics in this chapter derive from cover design suggestions, only some of which were finally used in the published pamphlets.

Printed by The Dolphin Press
(www.dolphinpress.co.uk)

Published by Happen*Stance*
21 Hatton Green, Glenrothes,
Fife KY7 4SD
www.happenstancepress.com

Orders
Further copies available for £4.00 (including UK p&p).
Please make cheques payable to Happen*Stance*
or order through PayPal on the website.
Further information: nell@happenstancepress.com

Foreword

IF YOU'RE A seasoned subscriber, you already know this is the ongoing story of Happen*Stance* Press, which began in 2005. It's an attempt to share the inside workings of the operation and tell some of the stories behind the publications.

In return for an annual subscription payment, subscribers are entitled to any chapbook of their choice and also the annual chapter of *The Story* (namely this publication, which has escaped out of 2009 and into 2010). They receive mailshots, too, from time to time with details of new publications and sometimes launches, events and so on. Most of the Happen*Stance* poets are themselves subscribers: it's an organisation for which good poetry readers are pivotal.

Happen*Stance* is an independent press: no form of funding underpins the work except the purchases of customers and the loyalty of subscribers (and sometimes donations from invisible but generous supporters). The publications are all modestly produced—they have to be. The aim is to achieve the best possible product on a very limited budget.

Up to now, there has been appreciative feedback from all sorts of people. Happen*Stance* even made it to the short-list of four pamphlet publishers listed in the new Michael Marks Award in 2009.

And the poetry does, I hope, represent a good range—very different writers accomplishing very different things. In 2008, the *Samplers* offered a new 'taster' publication, with a bit more biographical detail about the poet than usual. In 2009 there were the PoemCards (some people have enjoyed these who don't even *like* poetry). November 2009 also saw the start of the *Sequence* Series and the *Po-Lite* category.

For those of you who inhabit the online world with relish, I started to keep a publisher's blog on the website, updated each weekend. The *Sphinx* area of the website is also now hosting the most ambitious review scheme ever launched. I say this with confidence and slight trepidation: each of the pamphlets reviewed there receives feedback from at least three reviewers, and also gets a 'stripe' rating. Co-ordinating the whole thing is very complicated. It relies on dedicated service from a large team of doughty reviewers—more than thirty of them. There's lots of posting and packets involved, detailed interaction by email with the reviewers, an in-house edit to get all three correctly formatted and ready for posting on the web. It takes a very long time and the process is still developing and changing. I believe, hope, pray it's worth it. Let me know!

So things do keep changing. Many subscribers tell me they enjoy these chapters, that it *is* interesting to get a peep behind the scenes of this labour of love. I do hope so, because here I go again. . . .

1. The End of Study

Berowne: What is the end of study, let me know?
King: Why, that to know which else we should not know.
Berowne: Things hid and barred, you mean, from common sense?
King: Ay, that is study's godlike recompense.
[Shakespeare, *Love's Labour's Lost*, Act 1 Scene 1]

THIS CHAPTER SHOULD have gone out to subscribers in early December 2009, together with the Tooth Fairy Christmas card (which was in fact printed back in August). It didn't. I have studied to achieve these delays. I blame a lot on study.

I have a schedule every year (as well as a 'to do' list for every couple of months) and it's meant to keep me right. I thought this might be a good time to share such methods and so I went to dig out the schedule for 2009.

That's when I realised when things began to slip. It was this time last year (January) and *I didn't draw up the schedule*. Why? Because I had taken on an educational job in my other life which turned out to be monstrously time-consuming (more study matters). Because I had asked to have my teaching hours significantly reduced, and that didn't happen until some time in March, and even then the reduction wasn't as dramatic as intended. Because *Sphinx* took, as always, longer than I thought it would. Because I was awfully tired.

It's still interesting (to me, at least) to look back at the schedules. On the next page you'll find the one for 2008, a year in which I actually *did* achieve most of the things I had intended to do (in the publishing sense). At some point, but not always, I share the schedule with authors. I did this in 2008. Looking back on things, I see I did not do this (another Bad Sign) in 2009.

Mark Halliday and Sally Festing were carried over, metaphorically speaking, from 2008 to 2009, like small boats in a strong current.

But even the 2008 schedule on the next page makes no mention of the three *Samplers* I did in Summer of 2008, by Eleanor Livingstone, Andy Philip and Gill McEvoy (the series is still continuing). Nor of Colin Begg's *Nearly 'Nearly the Happy Hour'*, an MA dissertation (here presented as a delightful essay) that tells the story of how D A Prince's book-length collection was developed. It's available as a free download from the online shop.

Ever since I started, I have produced some publications (little usurpers) that weren't in the schedule. Not only that—each year there is at least one thing that *is* scheduled but doesn't happen, usually a poetry publication where another publisher offers a full-collection option to the poet (I regard this as a happy omission).

Then there are my wayward plans to make money for the press with things written by me (I don't have to pay myself or even be nice to the author.) *Fife Place-Name Limericks* is one of these. Since it may never ever materialise, I make passing mention of its notional existence here. Anyway, here's what was *meant* to happen in 2008:

Scheduling 2008

January	*Sphinx* 8 & D A Prince Nearly The Happy Hour
February	*Sphinx* 8 Start pamphlets by Janet Loverseed & Mark Halliday.
March	Post out *Sphinx* 8. Pamphlet: Marilyn Ricci.
April	Holiday first two weeks: catch up letters & reviews. STORY 2, winning entries to STORY competition
May	Publish NHH (D A Prince), *Rebuilding a No 39*, Marilyn Ricci, STORY 2
June	Publish Loverseed and Halliday.
July	Start pamphlets Martin Reed & Anne Caldwell.
August	*Sphinx* 9. Pamphlets Frances Thompson, Paula Jennings
September	Publish *Sphinx* 9, Thompson & Reed.
October	Publish Jennings & Caldwell. Start Sally Festing.: publication may go into 2009.
November	Write Chapter 3 of *HappenStance Story*. Xmas cards and mailshot.
December	Start *Sphinx* 10.

CHAPTER FOUR ▶ THE HAPPENSTANCE STORY

I seem to have established a pattern of working on publications in pairs: it makes sense to do all the promotional material for at least two at once, but it also means that each time I underestimate how long it takes to do flyers, review slips, registrations, review copies, updates on the website etc. More and more I see why publishers rely on poets to do their own promotion—especially in terms of organising launches and so on. Some even get their poets to post out the review copies. I haven't sunk that low yet!   Here's 2009:

Scheduling 2009

January	
February	
March	
April	
May	
June	Cliff Ashby *Sampler*, Sally Festing & Mark Halliday pamphlets. Start *Sphinx* 11.
July	Publish Ashby, finalise Festing, Halliday. Tommy McKean: Pitter *Conversation* pamphlet. Start pamphlets by Rose Cook, Alison Brackenbury.
August	Complete Cook and Brackenbury. STORY competition closes August 10: reading and shortlisting. Work on own second collection?
September	*Sphinx* 11.
October	Start STORY winning entries pamphlet. *More Unsuitable Poems*. Mark Halliday's *Flummery Festival?* Ruth Pitter *Conversation*.
November	*Sampler* Laurna Robertson? Pamphlets Clare Best, Deborah Trayhurn. Write *HappenStance Story* Chapter 4.
December	Start *Sphinx* 12. Pitter *Selected?* Soutar *Selected?*

7

No prizes for noticing the blanks between January and May. It was not that I did nothing then—I dealt with lots of submissions and reviews and brought out an issue of *Sphinx* too. However, I never got as far as drawing up a schedule, and if I had, my plans would have fallen apart.

In the end, Clare Best's lovely pamphlet *just* managed to be done before Christmas. Sally Festing, Mark Halliday, Rose Cook and Alison Brackenbury all saw the light of print in the same week—in September or thereabouts. Deborah Trayhurn was slightly ahead of Clare Best: hers was completed in late November. The *STORY* pamphlet was done at the same time as the unsuitable poems, this time titled *The Unread Squirrel* and they are, needless to say, by yours truly. There's no mention in the schedule of the PoemCards which materialised in the summer— because I didn't know I was going to do them. I can't remember when and how that idea came about, only that it did.

However, some of what is itemised, *didn't* happen, especially the prose. Chapter Four of the *Story* (you are reading it at this minute) was squeezed out. *Flummery Festival* was prose: it was to be the first in the 'Subtext' series which doesn't quite exist yet, and in any case Mark has placed it since elsewhere. Tommy McKean's interview with Ruth Pitter has been on the go for nearly two years now: it's on the long side for a pamphlet, but I very much want to share it with a reading public. In fact, I am working on it right now: the first draft has just gone off in the post to the poet's nephew and copyright holder for approval. And there *was* a sort of ambition to do a pamphlet *Selected* of both Pitter and William Soutar. Maybe. We'll see.

Before I start officially looking back over 2009, I'll look forward. Risky as it is, here's the schedule for 2010. There are actually a couple of other things I'm hoping to squeeze in, but I haven't dared to write them down yet, because already it's looking unrealistic. (Yes, there's a schedule for 2011 too but it's under wraps).

CHAPTER FOUR ► THE HAPPENSTANCE STORY

Scheduling 2010

January	Submissions, H-S Story Chapter 4, *Sphinx* 12.
February	Completing *Sphinx* 12 and reviews.
March	Ruth Pitter: *Conversation*. Robin Vaughan-Williams, *The Manager*. Publish and post out *Sphinx* 12. Start on pamphlets by David Ford, Jeremy Page.
April	
May	Complete Ford and Page pamphlets.
June	Start on pamphlets by Gill Andrews/ Gina Wilson
July	Submissions. Samplers by Patrick Yarker & Isobel Montgomery-Campbell. Start Kate Scott: pamphlet.
August	Finish Andrews/Wilson publications and Samplers.
September	Start Martin Parker (Po-Lite Series 2) and Tim Love: Pamphlet. Possibly Graham Austin (Po-Lite 3).
October	Finish Kate Scott's pamphlet. Holiday week mid month. Alan Hill, tanka, Sequence series 4 (to be out by early November)
November	Complete Kate Scott, Tim Love, Martin Parker.
December	Submissions month. Cliff Forshaw Sequence series 5, Jennifer Copley – *Living Daylights* Sequence series 6. Start *HappenStance STORY* chapter 5.

I have a little list (as Pooh Bah says in *The Mikado*) of other poets whose publications I'm hoping to do, some of them in 2011 and one or two perhaps even squeezed into 2010. But maybe not. When *Sphinx* reaches its final issue (12), it creates a little bit more time, but already its new online review function is phenomenally time-consuming and I'm currently well behind on that too. There's no mention of the STORY competition because there isn't going to be another one.

I spend a lot of time putting pamphlets into envelopes. Much of that

9

THE HAPPENSTANCE STORY ▶ CHAPTER FOUR

is thanks to you—that is to say you noble subscribers who not only re-subscribe each year but also purchase things. You can infer from the list of publications that financially it's hard to make this thing work (I'll come back to that shortly) and the subscriptions, the continued interest, the feedback, the modest purchases—this is what makes it viable. Without you, Happen*Stance* is sunk.

So thank you, thank you. You are patrons of the arts in the best and most fully appreciated sense.

2. *Sphinx* 10

Berowne: Subtle as Sphinx, as sweet and musical
As bright Apollo's lute, strung with his hair.
[Shakespeare, *Love's Labour's Lost*, Act 4 Scene 3]

THE FIRST PUBLICATION of the year was *Sphinx* 10 (the one with the bright yellow cover and black flyleaf). At one point I thought the tenth issue might be the last, but I decided to let the magazine run to issue 12 because there were still several interviews I wanted, a few more things to learn about. However, I had become trigger-happy. The chicken cartoons in this issue are actually *yellow*, which is how they're meant to look. (Doug Savage draws them on yellow post-its.) I had stuck to monochrome to keep the cost down, but by issue 10, since the magazine was losing money anyway, I decided I might as well be hung for a yellow chicken as a white one.

It was a nice issue anyway. It looked good. It has interesting interviews with editors of Nine Arches, Worple and Bluechrome, an interview with George Simmers (editor of the ezine *Snakeskin*) in heroic couplets and it also marked the launch of the *Sphinx* po-rating scheme. This grew from the idea that there ought to be—somehow—a way of making criteria for judging publications more visible. While the quality of poetry is inescapably subjective, some other things aren't—such as production quality, editing and so on. So the scheme invited reviewers to rate according to four criteria, only one of which was quality, and during the pilot I sent pamphlets to as many people as I could, on a sort of pass the parcel system.

It was very interesting. From this, it quickly became clear that anything receiving a 7 and above was pretty good. 6 was not half bad. 5 sat on the fence. Below 5 was a thumbs-down.

There was, however, substantial variation in ratings from different reviewers, proof (if any were needed) that our responses to poetry are anything but predictable. It convinced me that one review of a pamphlet could quite easily give a very skewed picture. And so things progressed to the new tripartite review (sometimes with comments from the Young Reader and/or The Common Reader too), together with a 'stripe-rating' (this appears as a *Sphinx* logo with a set number of stripes).

At first there were going to be ten possible ratings, but quickly I had to introduce half stripes. These look ridiculous. But there *is* a difference between 64% and 60%. The former gets six and a half stripes; the latter only 6.

I do worry about rating poetry in terms of tiger stripes. However, at least it's visually subtle, and some of the lower ratings are offset by strengths highlighted in the written reviews.

Already I've modified the rating criteria, too, to take account of reviewers' feedback. It's apparent that some reviewers are naturally high raters and some low. It's my plan to do some kind of standardisation system later this year, to help people be aware of how they're rating in relation to others (not to beat them into shape). Here are the current review criteria. The first three require intellect and reasoning, I think; judgement on the fourth is a matter for the heart.

Rating criteria	1 is low .... 10 is high
a) Production quality (paper, covers, 'feel' and design of publication)	1 2 3 4 5 6 7 8 9 10
b) Quality of the poetry.	1 2 3 4 5 6 7 8 9 10
c) Coherence of collection as a whole.	1 2 3 4 5 6 7 8 9 10
d) How warmly would you recommend?	1 2 3 4 5 6 7 8 9 10

CHAPTER FOUR ► THE HAPPENSTANCE STORY

You could argue that not all pamphlet collections are *trying* to be coherent, of course—but most readers sense whether or not even a brief collection seems to 'add up' to more than the sum of its parts. It is equally true, as George Simmers pointed out during the pilot, that some of the best poetry comes between the shabbiest covers. But in that case, the rating of production quality would be offset by full marks in the other categories.

Anyway, there it is—the system up and running on the website. More reviewers have had to be called in, of course, because although the number of pamphlets coming in for review is roughly the same, we now need three readers for each one. So I've been unashamedly exploiting the review capabilities of people who sent in poetry submissions this year, especially those who write particularly good covering letters. . . .

Interestingly, quite a lot of self-publishers have been keen to submit their work to this exacting review process, while some relatively professional publishers have sent nothing.

3. Cliff Ashby and Laurna Robertson: *Samplers*

King: How you delight, my lords, I know not, I,
But I protest I love to hear him lie,
And I will use him for my minstrelsy.
[Shakespeare, *Love's Labour's Lost*, Act 1 Scene 2]

Ever since HappenSTANCE published Cliff Ashby's *A Few Late Flowers*, I've been in correspondence with the author. From time to time, he sends a poem. How wonderful to be writing poems at 89 with sharpness and control undiminished! I loved some of the new ones. So I suggested a *Sampler*, to be brought out in time for Cliff's ninetieth birthday, comprising some new poems as well as a few gleaned from earlier books, one of which is below. It is an instant cure for sentimentality about womankind:

> The young women
> Do not wear flowers
> In their hair
> During the spring
> And summer
> Solstices
>   But all year round
> They spit
>   With great precision.
>
> [Cliff Ashby: *Sampler*]

The *Samplers* are modest productions but nevertheless the first four were on heavy-weight expensive card. The unit cost was alarmingly high and there was also a hitch with the printer: three sets came back untrimmed and had to be returned. So I decided to re-think. For Cliff's *Sampler* I went for a lighter weight card—and Robert at Dolphin Press took on the job for a much lower cost. I was pleased with the result of the look and feel, though this time I thought the paper weight was on the light side. Laurna Robertson's *Sampler*, done later the same year, was printed on the same card that we used for the cover of Mark

Halliday's *No Panic Here*. And that's the one we'll stay with, provided it continues to be available. One of the realities of the paper industry seems to be continuous change, especially when it comes to coloured papers or special qualities. You find something you think is gorgeous— and immediately they drop it from the catalogue.

Laurna Robertson's *Sampler* came about in a different way from any of the others. Hitherto, *Samplers* were for Happen*Stance* authors who were already, as it were, on the books. Laurna, however, approached me specifically with a *Sampler* in mind, and because her earlier pamphlet with Lapwing Press was no longer available, and because I'd met and liked her, I wasn't averse to the idea.

When I read the work, I became quickly enthusiastic. She writes with delicate humour and restraint—a distinctive style. We got the *Sampler* finished just in time for Christmas 2009 and Laurna was able to read and help Margaret Christie 'man' the Happen*Stance* stall at the Scottish Pamphlet Poetry Christmas Fair in Edinburgh.

> **Learning to Lie**
>
> prevarication first
>   *nearly ready just coming*
> and a vagueness, particularly with numbers
>   *not far not long not expensive*
> followed by evasion
>   *can't quite remember*
> and denial
>   *no, that's not what I said*
> then bluster
>   *you cannot believe I would do that*
> leading to the politic
>   *of course I will always love you*
> and at last to the boldest of all
>   *there is nothing to fear out there in the dark*
>
>   [Laurna Robertson: *Sampler*]

4. Rose Cook: *everyday festival*

Armado: Now, by the salt wave of the *Mediterraneum*, a sweet touch, a quick venue of wit! Snip, snap, quick and home! It rejoiceth my intellect. . . .
Shakespeare, *Love's Labour's Lost*, Act 5, Scene 1]

I BLAME GERRY Cambridge. His interview on typesetting for *Sphinx* 12 was disruptive. It led me to considering en dashes, em dashes and hyphens—not to mention the grave issue of hyphenation—in a depth I had never before thought possible. Today I even moved onto the issue of ellipsis. It's starting to drive me dotty. I have therefore returned to the business of trying to put words in their proper order, thereby to make sense. And what I intend to write about next is Rose Cook.

Rose heard about Happen*Stance* first when we reviewed a self-published pamphlet of hers in *Sphinx* 3 (see website archive). But she also came recommended by no other than Matt Harvey, a poet I would go a long way to listen to. She lives in the same town as Matt in Devon and she had done some Apples & Snakes gigs (I was able to listen to her on the web). She was even a member of a performance group bearing the wonderful name of 'Dangerous Cardigans'. So I knew right away she would be thinking about poetry in performance, that special significance of pause and emphasis, the quality that makes things work for an audience.

She sent her first submission in summer of 2007, and she got a reply from me which would have put a lot of people off. It read:

I like some of your poems very much, and I like the sound of you as a person as well. Now—as regards publication, this is difficult. I think I could probably work with you and that a good pamphlet would come out of it. There aren't yet, here, enough poems to move forward on (you'll see from my remarks in pencil that I like some much better than others), and I am horribly and complicatedly committed already next year. . . .

Most new poets are rushing. They want their book out as quickly as possible. They are off on the journey up Mount Olympus and they haven't got time to mess about.

But Rose wrote lovely letters, letters that showed she was a true, sane person who cared far more about achieving her best than getting there fast. She also believed I could help with that, and when we went on to work together, it was a good relationship. It is so hard to get the balance right between *interfering* with someone's poems (in a bad way) and encouraging them to make changes (in a good way) when you think changes would strengthen the text. I am always telling poets I am not God, even though I send out strong directives sometimes—I follow some kind of gut instinct developed from my own practice, I think. But gut instincts are not always right and each poet has to be the ultimate judge.

More and more I see where Happen*Stance* sits in terms of poetry publishing in general. It is somewhere between the Smiths Knoll mentoring scheme (a formalised arrangement) and the Poetry Business pamphlets (which go through an editing interaction after first placing in a competition). I work with a number of poets over a couple of years. There are exceptions to this, of course: some people send in poetry in a much more 'finished' state than others. Increasingly I've had approaches from established poets and one of the signs of being 'established'—whatever that dubious term really means—is that when you read the poems they strike you as having fully *arrived* (which is not the same as liking them).

If you're going to work with someone over a couple of years, that person has to feel like someone you could get on with over several cups of coffee. Why else would you do this at all? Rose immediately struck me as a lovely person. She subscribed to Happen*Stance* immediately and bought lots of publications (I am always pathetically grateful for this). And she went away and got on with the business of working at poetry, engaging in performance and generally building the connections which would make selling a pamphlet a reality.

I had told her I was horrendously busy (nothing changes). So she sent me a poem called 'A Poem for Someone Juggling Their Life' and I immediately took it personally, since if anyone is juggling—in the popular sense of too many balls in the air—it's me. There were others I particularly loved from the start ('Casting Off', which I have on the promotional flyer for this publication, was one of them). That sense of tenderness towards people, the sense that people are frail but lovable—that was something that appealed to me very much.

One of my early thoughts about that juggling poem was to have two of them as bookends. After all, it was a poem for someone juggling *their* life, not 'his' or 'hers'. There could have been his and hers versions, one at the start and one at the end. But the more I thought about it, the more I thought that poem should be referring to a woman—and yes, I know, that woman was *me*, but other women too, surely? So I suggested this to Rose, she agreed and the 'their' in the title became 'her'.

Later I put the juggling poem on one of the Happen*Stance* Poem-Cards (which hadn't been thought of at this stage) and it is the one that sells best on bookstalls. It crosses the divide between literary and popular writing. Readers who aren't 'poetry people' can like it. And that's one of Rose's gifts.

Her cover broke the mould as well. Usually I have normal bio on the back: a bit about the poet, a statement by me about the nature of the poetry. In Rose's case, we used a prose poem. But I must tell you how this came about....

When I send the first draft of the text to poets I always put something in the space on page 4 which can bear a dedication. Sometimes I write *for whomever* or *dedication can go here if you want one*. In Rose's case, I must have been feeling whimsical because I wrote *for my elephant*. What I didn't know was that she *had* written several poems about an elephant. That elephant was more than just a notion. So it was only when I said, "What about the dedication?" that she said, "I liked it" and I said, "What do you mean?" and she said, "I liked it being for my elephant" and I said....

You get my drift. I had *no idea* what she was talking about. So she sent me a couple of the prose poems she had done about her elephant. We changed the dedication to *for Tom (also for my elephant)* and we used one of the prose poems on the back cover instead of the bio. It is *sort of* biographical, with a twist. Because otherwise—although we had references to a pantomime horse inside the pamphlet (in another of my favourite poems)—there was little sign of the elephant. But there is now.

As always, the cover went through various possibilities: Gillian created more visual images than usual (it is a very visual set of poems). There was a juggling lady, a pantomime horse, birds in a tree (several) and we ended up with some of the birds: they pick up from a poem called 'The wagtail tree' but they also have a festival-ish look about them. The lack of capitalisation on the cover text is connected with the 'everyday' feel: these are not poems that set out to be 'important' or imposing. But they *are* celebratory.

THE HAPPENSTANCE STORY ▶ CHAPTER FOUR

The many and various graphics illustrate, I think, the sense of fun that collects around Rose's work, although she's not actually writing comic verse as such. In fact, there's quite a lot of sadness in this small collection of poems, and even that feeling when joy and heart-break co-incide, like the poem 'How close to breaking' which records that moment of seeing your child and experiencing, in the moment of love, the fragility of human beings, the reality of how easy it is to lose them:

How close to breaking

You were walking the promenade
towards me, carrying a ball and smiling.
Grief lurched into my heart
spreading like a bruise
so the dark cloud of starlings dancing
and the collapsed ballroom on the pier
and the punk strutting with his mouth studs
and cockerel hair glued into peaks
and the shepherd's delight sunset
all swam around our heads
and did not take the sadness away.

[Rose Cook: *everyday festival*]

5. Alison Brackenbury and the PoemCards

Armado: Arts-man, preambulate. We will be singled from the barbarous. Do you not educate youth at the chargehouse on top of the mountain?
       Shakespeare, *Love's Labour's Lost*, Act 5, Scene 1]

IN MY OTHER life I'm a teacher and I work in further education. That means I teach in what used to be called a 'technical college', though that term has been abandoned these days in favour of grander things. I teach literature some of the time and I work with individuals who mainly (there are exceptions) do not love Shakespeare and approach any kind of poetry with cordial distaste. So I'm in favour of the accessible, the work that moves, poetry that people can take to without the necessary armoury of a literary training. That isn't to say I don't like the other kind but it was one of the principles behind the PoemCards.

Another factor was the fact that Gillian, who does the graphic images on the Happen*Stance* poetry pamphlets, got married in summer of 2009. As her mother, not her father, I wasn't due to make a speech, but Gillian and Jamie (her fiancé) asked whether I'd like to read a poem during the registry office ceremony. I suggested 'A Metaphor Shared', by Mick Standen, a friend, poet and magazine editor who died suddenly in 2008. I'd always liked this particular poem and the way it sums up both the delight and difficulty of love.

They liked it too, so it was agreed I would read it. I thought it would be nice to give guests a copy (people don't remember poems well and some of them might have wanted to go back to it). For some time (inspired by Jenny Swann's Candlestick Press 'Instead of a Card' publications, as well as by some of the fine cards produced by Julie Johnstone at Essence Press), I had been thinking putting individual poems onto a proper card—not just a postcard. And although I'm an amateur at typography, I thought it would give me a chance to take something short and present it as beautifully as I could. So I decided Gillian's wedding poem could be a prototype. Lots of people *did* like this—they told me so—though some others no doubt thought I was potty.

Later I put together another six designs, one of which was the 2009

Christmas card. I've been doing poems on Christmas cards for a long time now, though none of them have been produced by a professional printer before with such a classy envelope! Although these are tiny little publications—just one poem each—you'd be surprised how long each one took to get to my satisfaction. I do like them, and I find them very useful too. However, it is at this point that my marketing and sales ability falls down, no matter how accessible the poems may be, since I haven't managed to get any of these into shops. There *are* places (particularly shops at museums and art galleries) where they would sell well, I believe, to casual purchasers. But I am juggling too many things. At present they're available on the web, which is probably not the best place to sell them.

One of the cards has an Alison Brackenbury poem on it, so that's a good link for me to move on to her pamphlet. Michael Mackmin was the first 'established' poet whose work I had the privilege of publishing. Alison was the second. We've corresponded for some years and she's also been a noble supporter of Happen*Stance* from the start, and a subscriber too.

She asked me whether I'd consider doing a chapbook collection of animal poems. There had been too many of them for her last book-length collection and she had wondered for some time whether they mightn't work together as a set. I had no hesitation about this. I love some of Alison's poems and I've always felt I *understand* the way she works. Some contemporary poets baffle me; she doesn't.

She is, however, modest beyond measure. Despite her evident success with readers, her approach was hesitant. It needn't have been. I jumped at the chance to work with her. When I refer to the set as 'animal poems', it sounds a bit like a zoo, or even a children's collection. It's not that. It's more that horses, cats, hedgehogs and sometimes other creatures tend to find their way into her work. They are part of her world. The theme of this pamphlet mirrors that—the delicate interaction between human existence and the other life forms on the planet. 'Shadow', the title poem, is about a kitten.

Does this seem sentimental? Poems about kittens and hedgehogs? The poems *are* emotive. Sentiment, however, is not uppermost. A few subscribers shared their fear that the collection might have been a bit

CHAPTER FOUR ▶ THE HAPPENSTANCE STORY

schmalzy, and then their subsequent pleasure in finding it was anything but. To me, this poetry of the natural world comes from an honourable tradition, to which Edward Thomas, Andrew Young and Robert Frost (to name just a few) also belong. But Alison also has Thomas Hardy's knack of creating a complex narrative in just a few words.

Let me talk a little bit about money now. Martin Edwards has just sent me a copy of his 1995 Redbeck Press pamphlet, *Coconut Heart*. Priced at £3.95 in 1997, it ran to 500 copies. *Five hundred!* In those days poetry must have been selling better than it does now. I've latterly reduced my print run from 300 to 250 and raised the cover price from £3.00 to £4.00. It doesn't save a lot of money to reduce by 50 (the first 200 copies generate the main cost) but it saves space in the spare bedroom (and trees). In Alison's case I maintained the print run of 300. Here's the breakdown of costs, roughly.

	Payment	Comment
Author	[£50.00 or £60]	Payment depends how much or little money is sitting in the account. Some poets take this in author-price copies (half the cover price). It is a notional payment and authors should be paid MUCH MORE. In this case, Alison took the payment in kind: 30 pamphlets.
Cover design	£50.00	
Print costs (300 copies of 32 page pamphlet)	£180.00	Price varies a bit according to weight of cover card or flysheet etc
Overheads: toner, paper for flyers, acetate sleeves, Jiffy bags etc	£40.00	Hard to be accurate about this: I am continually replacing toner.
Postage for sending out comp copies, promotional flyers and review copies	£40.00	Overall postage costs for the year are well over £1,000.00 so this may be a significant underestimate.
Approximate total:	£300.00	No cost in author payment

Of the 300 pamphlets, Alison took 'free' copies instead of an author's fee (and I understamped them in posting to her, but that's another

23

story). So that meant she took 42 copies to begin with, leaving me with 258 to sell. She then asked for 28 more, followed by another 30 (for which she paid), leaving 200. I sent out approximately 50 copies as review copies or comps to friends/ associates etc. That left 150. Many subscribers ordered copies at subscribers' price of £3.00 per copy (p&p is included) or as the 'free' copy included in their Happen*Stance* subscription, which makes things hard to calculate. There were quite a few orders by post also, at cover price, using flyer tear-off slips mainly distributed by the author. Through the website we've sold 19 to date; some of these will have been discounted to subscribers; others sold at full price. I have just counted and I have about 60 copies left.

So here are the sums:

Expenditure	Income	'Profit'
£300.00	Author copies: £116.00 Subscriber copies: £120.00 Other sales: £200.00 Total = £436	+ £136.00

Of the remaining copies, I keep six for my own records. The other 54 will sell, at various prices, so the income from them will, by the end of this year, have helped to offset the costs of other publications. *Salaams* and *everyday festival*, which were published at the same time (in a shorter print run), have sold nothing like that number of copies. I expect them to make a loss, even in the long term. Actually, I think *all* the other pamphlets from 2009 will lose money, with the possible exceptions of Clare Best's *Treasure Ground* and my own *The Unread Squirrel*. But there are reasons for that, which I'll come to later.

The aim is not to make a profit. The aim is to publish good poetry—some of it perhaps even minority-interest poetry. But one has to be sensible, and an author who is already doing readings and in a position to promote and sell the work is an enormous asset.

Alison uses Facebook to promote—she has a note on her profile page about *Shadow*. She has a 'fan club' too, through which she distributes occasional poems. She has a website, a very personal one. It's great.

Having said this, these things don't work for everyone. It is ironic in many ways that I'm praising Alison's promotional capabilities because she is naturally, I do believe, a reticent, self-effacing person. Even her promotional work is sensitive, gentle, never over-blown or pompous. And her poems are the same.

Animal hospital

Casualty 2454
was the hedgehog I found
heaving, grey-tipped spines collapsed,
heatstruck on the ground.

Each week I rang a voice.
He was 'lethargic', 'well'
or 'on a course of powders'.
His sharp grams rose and fell.

'Yes, you can take him back.'
'On Friday evening?'
                    'Sure.'
A mutter, like a rustled leaf.
'And can you take two more?'

Behind moist mounds of dog food
their boxes line the shed;
darker than quick dusk, one thrusts
a black and eager head.

Next day their beds are strewn aside,
Paper, meat—left. So soon.
I stand, a small lost animal,
beneath the daylight moon.

[Alison Brackenbury: *Shadow*]

6. Sally Festing: *Salaams*

Holofernes: The word is well culled, choice, sweet and apt, I do assure
you, sir, I do assure.
Shakespeare, *Love's Labour's Lost*, Act 5, Scene 1]

D<small>O YOU KNOW</small> there are poets who take *revenge*? In one recent case, a poet whose work I rejected has been bombarding me with regular poems by email. He presents them in a large bold font. Evidently I am meant to sit up and be startled by his talent. Another rejectee went on a tour of Scotland and emailed me daily extracts from his journal (I didn't read them). I have started to keep emails from mad poets because it's such an interesting phenomenon, though I do sometimes wonder whether I (and people like me) have driven them nuts.

Sally Festing was enormously patient with me. Other poets would have given up and gone away, or resorted to revenge tactics. Not Sally. She was persistent, courteous, charming and determined. She first approached me before I started keeping submissions records. It must have been in 2006, I think, because I have recorded the set she sent on 28 March 2007 as the second submission from her. My note is a little tetchy (I get irritable doing submissions. It's something to do with the pressure). I have noted "Sent a LOT of poems. She is good but she should put name and address on each one. And NOT number the pages. And not divide them into pamphlet sequences." I told her I wanted to hang onto them for the moment—

> Decision later but wd not be this year and likely selection
> from *both* sequences, not one or the other.

By this time I had divided the poems into a *Yes* set, a *Maybe* set, and some *No*s. There were 11 *Yes*es and 16 *Maybe*s. In a letter on 19th August, 2007 I suggested I was looking for at least 20 *Yes*es. I've also written:

> By this stage, I may have driven you demented. *What does it take to please this woman!!* But if not, hang on to the eleven I like, see what you can do with the *maybe*s, add any new ones you want considered, and send the result back to me.

Sally then adopted a colour coding system and she returned poems

Chapter Four ▶ The HappenStance Story

later that same month with little orangey-yellow dots at the top if they were *Yes* poems.

She also reacted to my unreasonable comment that I wasn't keen on poems inspired by pictures (or 'i.m.' poems) by including some of them anyway. By this time, I was working with D A Prince on her book *Nearly the Happy Hour* and Marilyn Ricci on her pamphlet *Rebuilding a Number 39*, and it turned out that Sally knew both these poets personally. So at least she understood how busy I was, because once again her own poems took a back seat.

Meanwhile, she kept subscribing, reading the publications and sending comments—something I valued enormously. And she was also busily working away at getting poems into the magazines, building the profile. Around Christmas, she sent for Ruth Pitter's *Persephone in Hades*. She wrote to say she had declaimed it aloud "thous and all—*isn't* Pitter good?" and ordered three more copies for Manningtree's Stanza group. Sally is generous in her appreciation of others, a true poetry enthusiast. In April 2008, she sent more poems and said she'd welcome comments. I'm pretty sure she didn't get any (comments). I was up to the eyes.

It wasn't until June 2009 that I finally sent her first draft. "I have left out a couple that I liked, in the interests of the coherence of the collection. A central binding theme is people / natural world (plants)," I wrote. (Sally is also prose author of *The Story of Lavender*.)

But in fact, one of the challenges was to find a set that would naturally hang together. Sally is moves in and out of different voices and methods. It's rare to find one poem that resembles another, in style or tone. She works on the texts tirelessly: by the end I had at least five versions of some. Painting *could* have been a connecting idea—but I ruled out a number of art-inspired poems because I have mixed feelings about these in general (some remain). And some of Sally's poems sometimes require close attention to penetrate what's going on beneath and between the lines (she's neither a light nor necessarily 'easy' read, and that is not a criticism). I'm going to include a poem which took me ages to work out, but it's become one of my favourites. Keep an eye on the different speakers and different indentations in 'Saturday Morning'.

27

Saturday Morning

He's drifting. Look   8.30 Birds

> She watches the thatcher,
> cap and white, flourish his yelmer,
> sprout wings and levitate—a harvest angel
> stabbed against pine trees in morning sun.

He's flying over our house. Where will he land?

> She sees the hands, small and vigorous,
> pull straw, pat, smooth with headrake,
> working to T-shaped pins. So finicky, it seems
> she has never looked properly before.

Can you see the man?

> It's Saturday. They shouldn't be in bed with
> books and breakfast and binoculars. He wonders
> about her marginally different view.
> Fumbling, she refocusses.

Are you watching the balloon?

> Hanging basket, burner-flares skim on air.
>   Birds chorus.

> She sees the glitter of speckled gold,
> a halo and two quick hands.

> [Sally Festing: *Salaams*]

7. Deborah Trayhurn: *Embracing Water*

Princess: Beauty is bought by judgement of the eye,
          Not uttered by base sale of chapmen's tongues. . . .
          [Shakespeare, *Love's Labour's Lost*, Act 2, Scene 1]

AND WHILE ALL these poetry pamphlets were going on, other things were simmering. *Sphinx* 11 was only one of them. Entering, and subsequently being short-listed for the Michael Marks award, was another. This was the first year of this competition. The Callum McDonald award in Scotland had first mooted the idea of rewarding publishers working in pamphlet forms. Michael Marks has picked up this idea, with two awards of £5,000, one for a notable poet, the other for a worthy publisher. And we were short-listed with three other small presses. This was encouraging.

To mark the event I went to the inaugural presentation in London. Happen*Stance* did not win (the prize was taken by Oystercatcher Press), but the word 'professional' was used to describe its operation. I was startled by this, having never felt fully professional at anything, but not displeased. Anyway, enough of that. It was back home and all hands to the pump, the poetry pump.

Deborah Trayhurn first contacted me by email. She had been put in touch by Linda Chase (whose work I knew and admired) and she had just won first prize in the Manchester Cathedral International Poetry Competition. Moreover, she lived not far away—in Perth.

I was a little uncertain, to be frank. One swallow doesn't, as they say, make a summer and one competition win (it was a *good* poem) doesn't necessarily mean there's a pamphletful to follow. However, I was very interested to know more, not least because Happen*Stance* is based in Scotland, with a commitment to support Scottish writers if and when it can. Most submissions, however, come from poets not working in this country. It is perfectly logical when you think the population of Scotland is so small . . . but at the same time you hope that now and again a really good new Scottish poet will come your way.

She sent a beautifully presented submission in early December 2008. My note records 'fussy punctuation'—again, this is me. I am often so unreasonable about these things. Anne Stevenson started it a long time ago when she was commenting on my own poems and told me that semi-colons and colons were prose punctuation, not poetry. I thought about this long and hard. I think she has a point. Poetry should have plain punctuation where possible, and although I don't absolutely rule out semi-colons, I do *scrutinise* their intent. And I like punctuation to be used consistently in poems. It's an interesting issue—when a line break or stanza break can serve instead of a comma. Such matters form the meat of email communications during publication processes. Perhaps it's not that important. To me, it is.

I gave Deborah detailed feedback and suggested she might send some more poems in July (I now have reading 'windows' twice a year which help to keep me sane).

I was moved and impressed by her second set. Though it was only a few months later, she seemed to me to have taken a dramatic step forward in terms of confidence. All the poems had first-line titles: this gave them a strong sense of unity, but so did other things. There was a powerful sense of 'voice' and method at work, a strong *flow* pushing through the set, like reading a river. I thought there was still a bit of work to do on punctuation and syntax but I was keen to go ahead and get a pamphlet out before Christmas. I liked the person behind the poems too. Her letters, with their rather strange, ripply handwriting had character. Their author was clearly self-effacing—and yet—well—*inspired*, I thought. These weren't workshoppy poems or poems written to order. They were flowing right out of her centre of self.

Now there's something else I need to say that I've forgotten. Life is so complicated. It is hard to remember how one arrives at a certain point, but in the middle of all this, there was a submission from one Robin Vaughan-Williams in Iceland. *Iceland*?! In my records I have written:

> Rather marvellous sequence of poems called *The Manager*, accompanied by an unusually business-like—almost too exemplary—covering letter. . . . His plans for promotion include *a tour*?! He has performed the sequence already in Leeds and Hoxton—says works well as performance material. Yes, I can see it would, though I have a few thoughts. But it's fun, it's lively, it's different, it's good. YES. But when?

CHAPTER FOUR ▶ THE HAPPENSTANCE STORY

I was so impressed by Robin's presentation of this work (let alone the work itself) that I wrote about it on the Happen*Stance* blog. This is part of what I said:

> I read this incredibly efficient approach with slight scepticism, the way you start listening to a remarkable new tenor thinking *he's good, he's good, but wait till he tries to hit that high note at the end of the aria.* I am only a pamphlet publisher. I don't usually get that quality of pitch. And if you create high expectation with your opening gambit, your poems have such a lot to live up to.
>
> However, they lived up. They did indeed. Shan't say more now, but it did remind me that doing this poetry job is exciting. Sometimes it's a whole set. Sometimes it's just one poem. But it does feel like panning for gold, with rather more gold than you could reasonably expect arriving through your letterbox.

The only thing that disappointed me in Robin's submission was the fact that he didn't seem to know anything about Happen*Stance*. But he does now.

Anyway, the reason I had to mention this at this point, midway through Deborah, is that Robin's *The Manager* was self-evidently a sequence. I like the fact that a pamphlet can do a sequence proud. Sometimes sequences get lost in book-length collections. So this gave me the idea that I would do a Sequence series with that in mind. And immediately I realised that Deborah's poems, each with their first-line titles, formed a natural sequence, a river of poems. And shortly after that, I decided the same was true of Clare Best. But I haven't got to that bit yet.

Embracing Water, Deborah's pamphlet, was the first in the Sequence series. I like many of these poems individually, but cumulatively they are electric. I like the tension between indoors and out, the clutter of urban life contrasted with open mountain landscape, the feeling that this is all primarily about love. 'In the absence of arcades' (overleaf) goes some way to illustrate this.

In the absence of arcades

and shopping malls, cinema
foyers, station halls, tunnels
of the underground, arches
and underpasses, bus-stop
shelters, deep doors, canopy
of an umbrella-ed crowd and
houses that lean together

out here, not wrap of darkness
nor even the odd tree stands
between you and me, and what
descends from the sky's mouth comes
from east west north or south—house
a carton in a tempest
and us leaning together.

[Deborah Trayhurn: *Embracing Water*]

CHAPTER FOUR ▸ THE HAPPENSTANCE STORY

7. Clare Best: *Treasure Ground*

Costard: No egma, no riddle, no l'envoy, no salve in the mail, sir. O, sir, a plantain, a plain plantain!
[Shakespeare, *Love's Labour's Lost*, Act 3, Scene 1]

I FIRST MET Clare in person at the Michael Marks award ceremony in London, another good reason for going. Her initial submission to me was in February 2008. She had been writer-in-residence at an organic farm in Lincolnshire. Her poems had been circulated to customers in their veg and fruit boxes—what an amazing idea! She took out a subscription to Happen*Stance* (another brownie point) and she sounded very nice. I responded to express interest but couldn't consider the poems until the July window. I finally wrote back to her in August of that year and my note records: "interesting sub—returned poems with detailed comment and a half offer. Send back in January."

Often what happens at this stage is the poet goes away and finds another publisher. Clare's work, and the central theme binding the poems, was very attractive. I thought she might well do this.

However, she didn't. She sent a second set in January 2009 and I noted in my book "beautifully presented. I think she is a goer." And almost immediately I knew this was another sequence. The poems follow the seasons just as the farming year follows the sun. The texts were crisp, succinct, clear, clean. What a lovely set: number 2 in the Sequence series. Again, the cumulative effect of the whole pamphlet is greater than the sum of its parts, although even individually some of these poems are potent.

We book-ended the sequence with prose pieces about the fens, which is where the poems are set. It makes the experience very personal, and that is right for these poems. I hope it might also attract a reader who is not necessarily the poetry type.

I said I'd come back to this pamphlet in terms of sales and this was also a print run which went the full 300. Andrew Dennis, who farms at Woodlands, the place which inspired these poems, asked for 1800 flyers to go out in vegetable boxes. He also ordered some pamphlets, sale or return, to take to farmers' markets. What a champion! Meanwhile,

33

Clare—who teaches for the OU and Brighton University, took her author's payment in copies. She purchased another 50 after that and then quickly ordered 30 more. A couple of people who had been at the launches she organised wrote, or emailed, to order additional copies for their friends. So she is doing magnificently. We have yet to see what happens overall, but I think there's a good chance this one will cover its costs. It is also particularly attractive: the flyleaves at front and back are a deep dark brown to mirror the colour of the Lincolnshire soil.

How to be Considerate to Sheep

When you're known to the sheep you meet,
put them at ease. Don't grimace or frown.

Provided they can see, sheep read expressions
just like you and me. Regular shearing

keeps fleece away from eyes. Horns
should not be allowed to grow too long.

Sheep perceive negative and positive emotion
so hang pictures of cheery faces

on the walls of the shearing shed or barn,
reassuring images for them to focus on.

These social animals will be less stressed
if the slaughterman's a stranger

than if it's someone they know. Please
encourage the unknown slaughterman to smile.

[Clare Best: *Treasure Ground*]

7. Mark Halliday: *No Panic Here*

Holofernes: This is a gift I have, simple, simple: foolish extravagant
spirit, full of forms, figures, shapes, objects, ideas,
apprehensions, motions, revolutions. These are begot in
the ventricle of memory, nourished in the womb of pia
mater, and delivered upon the mellowing of occasion.
But the gift is good in those in whom it is acute, and
I am thankful for it.
[Shakespeare, *Love's Labour's Lost*, Act 4, Scene 2]

MARK HALLIDAY IS not like anybody else. I first came across his work in *Poetry Review*, and since *No Panic Here* began to circulate, I've found other readers who remember those poems too and the way Halliday was championed by then *Poetry Review* editor Peter Forbes.

I have been corresponding with Mark for a number of years—ever since I was moved to write to him about those *PR* poems, in fact. He is a well-published American poet, with several collections under his belt, but no publication (until now) in the UK, though he has read to considerable acclaim at Aldeburgh and Snape.

He is often funny, almost invariably ironic. He writes in long, looping lines (hellish for a typesetter), following conversational rhythms. He's acutely self-aware, satirising the idea of Poetry's high horse of pomposity by leaping into the saddle himself. He pricks the bombast balloon bombastically. He makes you laugh. And yet, he's one of the most serious poets (serious about poetry) that I have known. Sometimes he is suddenly and sincerely sad.

I'm glad Mark allowed me to do this pamphlet. None of the poems inside have been published in book-form before. I fully expected readers either to love it or hate it. So far there has been only one reserved response: all the rest have been more enthusiastic than I dared to hope. *No Panic Here* is different from anything I've published before. Who but Mark would write a poem titled 'Ketchup and Heaven'? What a privilege to have been able to publish it. See next page for a taste.

35

Caveat: You must read the whole poem to get the full effect. This is only about half of it. The end is the best bit, but you have to earn the effect by reading all the rest. . . . So if you haven't already, send for the pamphlet.

Ketchup and Heaven

When you want ketchup on your French fries
and you upend the new bottle and nothing comes out
and you begin thumping the bottom of the bottle
with the heel of your palm till it hurts
and the restaurant staff and clientele glance at you
with mild disdain for your vulgar *and* ineffectual Stone Age
                                                           behavior,
you know you are not in heaven.

Heaven is going to be a place where the ketchup flows freely,
like milk and honey in the rivers,
and you won't have to stick your knife in
and wiggle it vigorously till at last
the seduced ketchup consents to blurt out
in gobbets larger than you intended
on the lip of your plate. Heaven will in fact be
a place where you don't even need ketchup,
because the French fries will already be somehow
sufficiently flavorful and interesting in their own right . . .

[from 'Ketchup and Heaven' in Mark Halliday's *No Panic Here*]

7. Unread Squirrels, Managers & Conversation

Rosaline: Nay, I have verses too.
 [Shakespeare, *Love's Labour's Lost*, Act 5, Scene 2]

I DON'T WANT to say a lot about *The Unread Squirrel*. It is a follow-up to the first Happen*Stance* publication in 2005 (*Unsuitable Poems*), and it's subtitled 'More Unsuitable Poems' because it seems to me they might *be* more unsuitable than the first lot in several ways. One is titled 'How to Piss Off Your Prospective Poetry Publisher' (a verse companion piece to *How (Not) to Get Your Poetry Published*). The poems are a motley array and the last one isn't even funny, though it's hard to know what kind of book it *would* suit. But as with Ruth Pitter, my comic side insists. Perhaps it's a necessary counterpart to the very much darker poems which will be in a book forthcoming from Shoestring Press hopefully later this year. At present that's titled *Plot and Counter-Plot*.

Should anyone wonder how I manage both my own poetry and Happen*Stance* as well, the answer is I don't. Happen*Stance* has saved the world from several onslaughts of H. Nelson. *Plot and Counter-plot* has been nearly a decade in the making, and the Unsuitables have sprung up, from time to time, like persistent weeds in a garden forcing their way through.

Earlier, I talked a bit about finance. Each person who works on poetry publications has a different way of funding this commitment: some have a pension, or an alternative income, or a substantial backer. They may be running several businesses and the others somehow keep the poetry side going. I am lucky I have another job educating youth at the charge-house in Kirkcaldy. It creates a conflict of interest sometimes, but it pays the bills.

The Helena Nelson side, however, directly subsidises the poetry. Happen*Stance* has never had Arts Council Funding and my attempts to apply for assistance with *Sphinx* were unsuccessful. In an indirect way though, I *have* had financial assistance from government funds. Most years I do a couple of poetry readings in my Helena Nelson capacity (the new pamphlet will go with me to these) and mainly those are paid. The payment, whichever group is making it, almost invariably

37

draws on Arts Council support. The money goes straight into Happen*Stance*. I did some work for Scribner's last summer—a monograph on the Scottish poet William Soutar—the payment went into Happen*Stance*. In the last financial year, Happen*Stance* made a much bigger loss than usual (there are various reasons for that which I won't go into here) and so I will get a tax rebate from my other paid income. The rebate will pay for the final edition of *Sphinx*. Which is just as well because it will be an expensive one.

The outgoings on Happen*Stance* each year are roughly £8,000. That means I need to pull in the same amount from various places. The subscriber list is crucial (that's you). I'm convinced the key for the future lies in building the subscriber base. It's not just a matter of money. Well, it *is* a matter of money—but also much more than that. Subscribers don't just fork out; they also *read*. What poets and publishers need more than anything else is people who will buy and *read* the poetry. Otherwise what would be the point?

Of course there's too much poetry in the world for anybody to read their way through, too much straw to spin into gold. In one sense, we're swamped with the stuff. I do have moments (confession time) when I think I never want to see another poem again (especially when it's one in bold font by email from a revenge poet). It's like music. The world is full of it, gloriously full. There are lots of tunes but you need to keep listening until you find a true melody—true and beautiful. When you do, it sustains you like nothing else.

Some of *my* favourites are in the Happen*Stance* publications. I grew up with Ruth Pitter. Often classed as 'neo-Georgian', she might feel a little rhymey for the modern taste. Her *Collected* volume can be overwhelming too, because it is so full, and some of the work does feel old-fashioned. But at her best, as they say, at her *best*, she is second to none. When I brought out her long poem, *Persephone in Hades*, in 2007, I had an unexpected letter from an American purchaser who had tracked it down on the net. Thomas McKean had the most beautiful handwriting. He wrote to tell me he had known Ruth personally over a number of years. He had edited a slender (and limited) Enitharmon edition of her work issued in the 90s (*A Heaven to Find, Uncollected Poems*). We corresponded. It transpired he had recorded an interview with her

which had never been published:
> I've never managed to place this interview with Ruth I've mentioned to you; it is rather long but good. More of a conversation, really, as she was quite old when it took place and I didn't want to press her; also, by that time we'd become friends which naturally changes the tone of it all.

Naturally I asked to read it. It was at the back of my mind to look for a magazine outlet (friendly editors I have known) but it was too long. It was too long for a pamphlet too really but . . . well, it has materialised.

Alan Dixon, artist, friend and poet, who did the magnificent woodcut on the cover of *Persephone in Hades* for no payment whatsoever, sent me several more woodcuts to choose between. The one of a cat best fitted the cover. I love the cover and I love this *Conversation*. Only Ruth Pitter could call a fellow poet "a rumptitoo old cuss". She was a character and a half. Ideally I would have liked to bring out a pamphlet selection of her poems at the same time, and there *is* a plan underway for that, but I simply can't fit it in. Yet.

Financially speaking, *A Conversation with Ruth Pitter* is another insane publication. The chances it will cover its costs are remote. But think of the privilege. If Happen*Stance* doesn't do it, who will ever read this? And who, having read it, could not feel enriched?

Two more things to mention. First, there's this year's STORY, the anthology of winning entries to the competition. It was a delight and a surprise to find that two of them (Fiona Thackeray and Heather Reid) were based near Perth, members of Ajay Close's writing group. They even knew Deborah Trayhurn personally. It is lovely working on stories for a change, and these were good ones. Another of the winners was Tom Bryan, well known Scottish poet and author. So although most of my *poets* in 2009 had small connection with Scotland, the STORY pamphlet was rich in this regard. It is unlikely, however, that we'll run it again. The time investment, relative to the income generated, is not sensible. We've learned a lot from the experience, and Sarah Willans (Competition Administrator) and I had some rare old telephone discussions about the entries too, but it's the end of that 'chapter'—and nearly the end of this one too.

So I'll end with some poetry. I mentioned Robin Vaughan-Williams'

THE HAPPENSTANCE STORY ▶ CHAPTER FOUR

The Manager earlier (page 30). This was the young man who so impressed me with his approach, and subsequently with his wry, funny, surreal, professional, unusual sequence. *The Manager* is a tale for our times if ever there was one. It's good. It's very good. It is a sequence, of course, so no single extract will do it justice, but just to give you the flavour . . .

MANAGER #2
Photobooth

The manager sits behind blue curtains,
rattles the stool, flattens his tie,
and waits.

In a moment of reflection
he sees the white light shine through the back
of his dimly lit head. Infrared

steals over fingers,
flashes blood,
scans his brain.

The number is endless, indecipherable.
He does not know how much he is worth.

[Robin Vaughan-Williams: *The Manager*]

After you've read this chapter, do pass it on, or even use the flyer to recruit another subscriber to the ranks. Just as (according to Rosaline) "A jest's prosperity lies in the ear / Of him that hears it, never in the tongue / Of him who makes it", so the good fortune of Happen*Stance* publications lies less in what *I* put on the pages than in what you take out. Love's labour is never truly lost, is it? Thank you, subscribers. Thank you again.